A Gift To:

_____

From:

_____

Wisdom From Ole Time Jamaican People

Lessons From Jamaican Proverbs

Veronica V. Sutherland

DEDICATION

This book is dedicated to my ancestors who were channels of the wisdom of "Ole Time People". Special dedication to my mother, her parents and siblings.

INTRODUCTION

Jamaican culture is a melting pot of several cultures, mainly African and European. The proverbs are no different they are derived from a number of cultures mainly African and European

Older Jamaicans will recall their parents or older persons saying; "ole time people use to sey ..." You would stop whatever you were doing as you knew that it would be followed by a proverb which was meant for you to stop your activity and to teach you a lesson you should not forget.

The proverbs are written in the Jamaican language. All pronunciations are phonetic. An English translation is done as precisely as possible, followed by the meaning of the proverb.

Veronica has attempted to give a brief insight into the lessons that may be learnt from these proverbs. She completes each with an action step you can take to cement these lessons in your lives.

Jamaicans as you read, reminisce about your childhood in the 'good old days'. Friends of Jamaica imagine yourself in a Jamaican home with your parents or grandparents uttering these proverbs to guide your actions.

ACKNOWLEDGEMENT

I must say thanks to my husband for editing this manuscript. Thanks also to my friends who offered encouragement.

I must also express appreciation for those individuals who allowed me the chance to be bilingual at a time when English was the only language expected of educated Jamaicans.

Proverb: A noh di same day leaf drap a riba battam ih ratten

English: It is not the same day the leaf falls to the bottom of the river it rots

Interpretation: A person may wait a long time to avenge someone who has hurt him

What can you learn?

When a person is hurt they do not always react in a hurt manner immediately. Some persons sit and plot their revenge for days, months or years. If you have done anything that may have hurt someone, apologise as quickly as possible and ensure that your actions from then on are in alignment with the apology. This may help to defuse the situation.

Your Response:

Apologise to someone your words or actions may have hurt

Proverb: A noh ebry mango gat maggige

English: Not every mango has maggots

Interpretation: Not all persons are corrupt

What can you learn?

We all have good and faulty characteristics but faulty characteristics in a person do not necessarily make a person bad. Look for the good in the persons you meet.

Your Response:

Highlight the good qualities of your family, friends and acquaintances and downplay their faults.

Proverb: A noh ebryting fram above a bless'n

English: Not everything from above is a blessing

Interpretation: Not all influential persons bearing gifts have your best interest at heart

What can you learn?

When your superiors give you rewards accept them graciously but beware that these gifts are meant to disarm you so that they can take advantage of you.

Your Response:

Examine the motives of those persons who bring you gifts, being careful not to go on a witch hunt.

Proverb: A noh ebryting good fi it good fi tawk

English: Not everything that is good to eat is good to talk about

Interpretation: Not all experiences are fit to talk about

What can you learn?

Some experiences are for personal reflection and are not meant to be shared with all and sundry.

Your Response:

Reflect on those experiences that have taught you some deep lessons.

Proverb: Bad luck wos dan obeah

English: Bad luck is worse than witchcraft

Interpretation: A person who is always experiencing adversity feels that the severity is worst than it would have been had it been witchcraft

What can you learn?

> You experience adversity because of actions you take, usually as a reaction to some factor over which you have no control. Think carefully before making decisions as they can have far reaching consequences.

Your Response:

In the midst of adversity ask yourself:

- *What did you do right and would not change?*
- *What could you have done differently in order to avoid the adversity?*

Make a note of these to guide you in the future.

Proverb: Bowl goh, packy come

English: Bowl goes, gourd comes

Interpretation: When you do a favour for a person they will in turn do a good deed for you

What can you learn?

> When you do a favour for a person they feel obliged to do a favour for you. This is so especially if they thing you did it out of genuine love and expects nothing in return.

Your Response:

> *Find ways of serving your neighbour by filling a need he/she has but expect nothing in return.*

Proverb: Cack mout kill cack

English: Cock mouth kill cock

Interpretation: Our own words cause us harm

What can you learn?

> We should be careful in what we say as our utterances can come back to haunt us.

Your Response:

> *Speak positive and uplifting words at all times.*

Proverb: Carry goh, bring come

English: Carry it to and bring it back

Interpretation: To gossip (Stories go and come)

What can you learn?

Be careful not to take mischievous stories from one person to the next. It is unkind to spread rumours about others. Person's lives can be destroyed by stories being spread for which there is no proof.

Your Response:

Before you repeat something you have been told ask yourself the following questions:

- *Is it true?*
- *Is it kind?*
- *Will it build relationships?*

Proverb: Chicken merry hawk deh near

English: The chicken is merry, the hawk is near

Interpretation: In the midst of our joy there is danger

What can you learn?

When celebrating or frolicking we should not be frivolous but should be conscious that a threat could be lurking nearby.

Your Response:

Practice soberness in your celebrations and merrymaking.

Proverb: Cowad man kip soun bone

English: Coward man keeps sound bones

Interpretation: Avoiding fights can preserve a person's wellbeing.

What can you learn?

> Never brazenly stand up to anybody when you are in danger of being seriously hurt or killed. It is better to walk away from these situations than to end up unnecessarily hurt.

Your Response:

> *Practise counting to ten, to diffuse situations that can escalate to your doing or saying something, that may hurt you or someone else.*

Proverb: Dem gih yu baskit fi carry wata

English: They gave you a basket to carry water

Interpretation: You are not given the resources to do the job

What can you learn?

> Always be prepared to do a task assigned or you could find that you are unable to carry it out.

Your Response:

> *Always be prepared.*

Proverb: Di ola di moon, di brighta ih shine

English: The older the moon, the brighter it shines

Interpretation: The older a person is the wiser he is

What can you learn?

Older people have seen many moons and therefore have seen and experienced many happenings. These various experiences would have taught them many lessons from which you can learn.

Your Response:

Sit with an older person and have a cool drink or cup of tea and talk about life. You will come away with a number of gems you can use in your life.

Proverb: Di same knife stick ih sheep stick ih goat

English: The same knife stick the sheep will stick the goat one day

Interpretation: When you are planning harm for someone else, it could turn around to you.

What can you learn?

Do good and good will follow you. Always try to be kind and compassionate to others and others will be kind and compassionate to you and your family.

Your Response:

Be kind to those persons who are unkind to you.

Proverb: Duppy know who fi frighten

English: A ghost knows who to frighten

Interpretation: Powerless people will intimidate those they perceive to be less powerful than them

What can you learn?

Persons that see you as a softy will try to get the better of you. Be prepared to stand up for yourself without resorting to physical or verbal fighting. When you are in a more powerful position than someone else, treat them as you would want to be treated.

Your Response:

Find out one good quality about your subordinates each week.

Proverb: Ebry Dawg gat im day, ebry puss im 4 o'clock

English: Every dog has his day, every puss his 4 o'clock

Interpretation: Everyone has their time to excel or be in the limelight

What can you learn?

Don't be jealous of the person who seems to be succeeding today, you too will have your time to shine.

Your Response:

Make a list of your talents and find a way of sharing them with your community.

Proverb: Ebry mickle mek a muckle

English: Every mickle makes a muckle

Interpretation: Every little bit adds up

What can you learn?

Saving steadily towards the accomplishment of a major goal will get you there rather than waiting for the time when you will have a lump sum. Saving a small amount steadily over time will accumulate much.

Your Response:

Set a major goal and decide how much money you need to save weekly or monthly over a period of time.

Proverb: Ef yu han inna lian mout tek time tek ih out

English: If your hand is in the lion's mouth, remove it slowly and carefully

Interpretation: Be cautious in getting out of difficulties/troubles

What can you learn?

Never try to remove yourself from a difficult situation before weighing the pros and cons. Being hasty in your decision could result in more harm than good.

Your Response:

List the consequences of the solutions you may have for a difficult situation you are facing. Formulate a plan to solve the problem.

Proverb: Ef yu lidung wid dawgs yu wi rise wid fleas

English: If you lie with dogs you will rise with fleas

Interpretation: You will pick up the bad habits or misfortune of the people you associate closely with

What can you learn?

Be careful of the friends you keep as you will pick up their habits. Associate with positive persons so that you will acquire positive habits. Avoid negative persons who will drain your spirit.

Your Response:

Associate with positive people who will build you up..

Proverb: Finga neber sey look ya im sey look yanda

English: Finger never says; "look here", he says; "look yonder"

Interpretation: People never call attention to their own faults but will always point to other people's faults

What can you learn?

It is human nature to ignore our own faults while drawing attention to the faults of others. We should seek to know and to correct our own faults at all times. We should never speak evil of others but if our friends or acquaintances have habits that are offensive or harmful to them or others, speak to them in love about these habits.

Your Response:

Look for the good in each person you meet.

Proverb: Fiyah deh a muss muss tail im tink a cool breeze

English: A fire is at the mouse's tail but he thinks it is a cool breeze.

Interpretation: Danger lurks but we unsuspectingly miss the signs until it is right upon us

What can you learn?

> Sometimes we think our actions are leading to success, when in fact they are leading to our destruction. We should be aware of our environment at all times and act in a manner that will lead to harmony and not discord.

Your Response:

> *Do good at all times and do not try to manipulate situations for your gain at the expense of others.*

Proverb: Good frien betta dan packit money

English: A good friend is better than pocket money

Interpretation: A good friend is worth more than our material possessions

What can you learn?

Our good friends are always there for us and are valuable whether we are in or out of trouble. We should therefore treasure our friends and treat them well whether or not we are in need of help.

Your Response:

Call a friend you have not spoken to recently.

Proverb: Craben choke puppy

English: Craven or greed chokes puppy

Interpretation: Greed will hurt you

What can you learn?

> Don't be greedy or overly ambitious as you may end up hurting yourself.

Your Response:

> *Do everything in moderation.*

Proverb: Hog sey fus wata yu si, wash

English: Hog says; "the first water you see, wallow"

Interpretation: Make use of the first opportunity you get

What can you learn?

When you get an opportunity to do something, don't ignore it and go searching for a bigger and better one. There is no guarantee that you will get a similar opportunity much less a better one in the future. More times than not that first small opportunity leads to more beneficial opportunities.

Your Response:

Embrace the daily opportunities you get, giving thanks to God for each one.

Proverb: Howdy an tenky noh bruk noh square

English: Hello and thank you will break no square

Interpretation: To say hello and thank you will bring no harm

What can you learn?

You can make more friends than enemies by being nice to people. Saying hello and thank you will endear you to others. It makes for better relationships with those persons with whom you interact.

Your Response:

Say hello with a smile to those persons you come in contact with daily. When someone does something for you or pays you a compliment say: "thank you" with a smile. Watch your world light up as people respond in like manner to you.

Proverb: If yu cyaa tan di heat, get outta di kitchin

English: If you cannot stand the heat, get out of the kitchen

Interpretation: If the pressure is too much, leave the situation

What can you learn?

Stressful situations can cause you to get sick, so if you are too stressed in a situation it is best to leave or get help.

Your Response:

Learn to recognize when you are approaching breaking point due to stress and take a break.

Proverb: Ih betta fi lose yu time dan yu characta

English: It is better to lose your time than your character

Interpretation: It is better to keep your principles than to try to save time

What can you learn?

> A good character is better than material worth. Your character is the essence of who you are and should therefore be a positive promotion of you.

Your Response:

> *Think about the qualities you want the world to associate with you. Take steps to ensure these are the qualities you promote through your actions.*

Proverb: Jump outta fryin pan inna fiyah

English: Jump out of the frying pan into the fire

Interpretation: In your bid to escape one problem you end up with a bigger one

What can you learn?

> Never run away from your problems. Face them head on and try to find a solution. Running away usually makes them worse, as well as adding more problems to those you already have.

Your Response:

> *Discuss possible solutions with the other persons affected by the problem.*

Proverb: Kin teet kibba heart bun

English: Smile to cover heartache

Interpretation: Smile in the midst of your troubles

What can you learn?

Not everybody has to know when things are not okay with you. Smile and behave as if you are happy even when your whole world is upside down.

Your Response:

Smile at everyone everyday whether or not you feel like it.

Proverb: Lang run, shaat ketch

English: Long run, short catch

Interpretation: Although you may run for a long period of time after wrongdoing, you will be caught someday

What can you learn?

> Own up to your wrongdoing. You may be able to hide what you did for a while but you will be caught, usually when you least expect it.

Your Response:

> *Confess to something you have been hiding for a long time. Savour the exhilarating feeling of freedom you experience.*

Proverb: Laud tek di case an gi mi di pilla

English: Lord take the case and give me the pillow

Interpretation: I can't deal with this problem so Lord you solve it

What can you learn?

> We sometimes feel overwhelmed by our problems. It is quite okay to seek help from a power higher than ourselves. Pray to God for clarity and discernment to find solutions.

Your Response:

> *You have a problem – pray to God to reveal the solution. Stay calm and listen so that you will not miss His response.*

Proverb: Mannas tek yu roun di worl

English: Good manners will take you around the world

Interpretation: You will go places with good manners

What can you learn?

A person with good manners will gain the respect of others. People will feel comfortable in your presence as they will feel they can trust you. This trust will lead them to treat you in a manner that will propel you to higher heights.

Your Response:

Treat all people you meet with respect.

Proverb: Man noh ded noh call im duppy

English: If the man is not dead do not call him a ghost

Interpretation: As long as a person is breathing, he is capable of achieving something useful

What can you learn?

> Do not write-off people because they do not meet your standards or seem hopeless. Once there is life there is hope and with encouragement and the needed resources anybody can succeed.

Your Response:

> *Encourage someone who has failed to reach a goal.*

Proverb: Mischief come by di poun an goh by di ounce

English: Mischief comes by the pound and goes by the ounce

Interpretation: A mischievous person can cause a lot of trouble which is difficult to curtail

What can you learn?

> Make love not war. When we cause trouble it may not be easy to reverse. The hurt caused could be permanent or take a long time to heal.

Your Response:

> *Love your neighbour as yourself.*

Proverb: Mi use to di hengin di chokin woan kill mi

English: I am used to the hanging so the choking will not kill me

Interpretation: I am used to hard times or difficulties so small inconveniences will not affect me

What can you learn?

> Do not despair when you find yourself in a difficult situation. Examine the problem and find the areas you can find a solution for and fix them. Stop worrying about those areas you have no control over. They will still be there whether or not you worry.

Your Response:

> *Break your problem into manageable areas and solve each area one step at a time.*

Proverb: Monkey mus know weh im a goh put im tail, befoe im orda trouses

English: The monkey must know where he will put his tail before he orders a pair of trousers

Interpretation: You must know if what others are doing is suitable for you before you decide to do likewise

What can you learn?

> Don't follow fashion for the sake of being in style. Be conscious of your qualities and seek to do those things that will complement you.

Your Response:

> *Let your actions be consistent with your true self.*

Proverb: Neva si come si

English: Never see, come see

Interpretation: A person shows off because they are not used to having what they now have or to be in the situation they are now in.

What can you learn?

> There is no need to show off if you have been blessed with things you did not have before. They should be enjoyed in humility.

Your Response:

> *Give thanks for your blessings.*

Proverb: Noh buy puss inna bag

English: Do not buy a puss in a bag.

Interpretation: Inspect anything you purchase or accept from other people

What can you learn?

Do not be caught unaware in any situation. Ensure you are getting what you pay for when buying goods and services. Look at the product carefully. Persons presenting themselves to you should be thoroughly investigated before you accept them as being authentic.

Your Response:

Examine all goods and services you purchase to ensure they are what you really want and that they are in good condition.

Proverb: Noh care how boar hag try fi hide unda sheep wool, im grunt gi im wey

English: No matter how much the boar tries to hide under sheep wool, his grunt always betrays him

Interpretation: No matter how much people pretend to be what they are not, their true self will come out

What can you learn?

> Pretending to be someone you are not is futile. You cannot keep up the pretence forever and sooner or later someone will discover who you really are. You are one of a kind, made for a unique purpose, do not deprive the world of the true you.

Your Response:

> *Be yourself in all situations and let your uniqueness shine.*

Proverb: Noh heng yu baskit weh yu cyaa reach ih

English: Do not hang your basket where you cannot reach it

Interpretation: Do not live above your means

What can you learn?

To be successful in life you should live within your means. Do not spend more than you earn. In other words do not borrow as you will be beholden to the lender.

Your Response:

Make a budget based on your income and stick to it.

Proverb: Noh mug noh bruk, noh cawfi noh dash wey

English: If the mug is not broken the coffee will not throw away

Interpretation: In life, secrets only become known when relations are broken

What can you learn?

When relationships become sour, the untold stories become known. Look carefully at what you do in relationships for it may come back to haunt you. Nurture your relationships so that they will remain intact. Live your life so that you will have nothing to hide.

Your Response:

Each morning pledge to be positive in all your dealings with others.

Proverb: Ole fiyah tick easy fi ketch

English: Old fire sticks are easy to ignite

Interpretation: It is easy for two people, who were once intimately involved, to revive the relationship

What can you learn?

Bonds formed in relationships are not easily broken or forgotten therefore cherish the relationship you currently have.

Your Response:

Be kind and loving to your partner.

Proverb: One han wash di ada

English: One hand washes the other

Interpretation: A good deed is repaid with another good deed

What can you learn?

> One good turn deserves another. We cannot live without the help of our neighbour. Relationships are built when we do favours for or help each other.

Your Response:

> *Do a good deed for your neighbour and watch how your relationship deepens as they lookout for you.*

Proverb: One one coco full baskit

English: One coco at a time will fill the basket

Interpretation: You achieve your goals one step at a time

What can you learn?

Rome was not built in a day, so you should not expect that you will become successful overnight. Work steadily towards achieving your goals.

Your Response:

1. *List your goals.*
2. *List the steps you need to take to achieve them.*
3. *Follow these steps and adjust as needed.*

Proverb: Patient man ride dankey

English: A patient man rides a donkey

Interpretation: Much can be accomplished by being patient

What can you learn?

> Patience is a virtue that will bring success. Impatience will result in wasted time and other resources through mistakes made in the rush to get things done.

Your Response:

> *Give yourself enough time to get things done slowly savouring the process and the product.*

Proverb: Pit inna di sky ih fall inna yu yiye

English: If you spit in the sky it will fall in your eye

Interpretation: If you hurt others or wish them evil you could be paving the way for your own letdown

What can you learn?

> Be careful what you wish for others, it may surely happen to you. Wish and do good to others and good will follow you.

Your Response:

> *Identify five persons and pray that the desires of their hearts will be fulfilled.*

Proverb: Puss awn dawg noh hab di same luck

English: Puss and dogs do not have the same luck

Interpretation: What some people will get away with, others will not

What can you learn?

> When you decide to carry out an activity do so because it is right for you; not because someone else is doing it.

Your Response:

> *Look for five ways to appreciate yourself.*

Proverb: Puss bruk cwocnat inna yu yiye

English: Puss broke a coconut in your eye

Interpretation: Your eyes suggest something devilish is afoot

What can you learn?

Your eyes can tell the world much about you. Ensure your intentions are well meaning in all your interactions, as people tend to confirm that the message in the eyes match that from your lips and body.

Your Response:

Look in the eyes of others when speaking to them to show that you have nothing to hide.

Proverb: Rack stone a riba battam noh know sun hat

English: A stone at the bottom of the river does not know the heat of the sun

Interpretation: A sheltered life does not prepare you for hard times

What can you learn?

You should be aware of what is happening around you. Parents do not shelter or spoil your children in such a way that they cannot function in new situations in which they find themselves.

Your Response:

Have a conversation with a street person about life.

Proverb: Sarry fi mawga dawg, mawga dawg tun roun bite yu

English: Sorry for a meagre dog and the meagre dog turn around and bite you

Interpretation: The person you helped when he was in need acts ungrateful or hurts you when he is ok

What can you learn?

> When you do a good deed for someone, do not expect anything in return. When you practice to help people someone will help you when you are in need, usually someone you did not help.

Your Response:

> *Do good to those people from whom you have no expectation of repayment.*

Proverb: Scawnful dawg nyam dutty pudd'n

English: Scornful dog eats dirty pudding

Interpretation: Picky people will unknowingly partake of or participate in less than wholesome things

What can you learn?

> There is no need to nitpick. When you accept things and people as they are you will get along better with them. Your life will harmonize with those of the people in your sphere of interaction.

Your Response:

> *Imagine yourself as a less fortunate individual. Walk yourself through a day in their life. What can you do to make a difference in that person's life? Pledge to make this difference.*

Proverb: Sick noh cyah, dacta noh cyah

English: Sick does not care, doctor does not care either

Interpretation: If you do not care about yourself others will not care either

What can you learn?

Practice self-sufficiency so that when you have a problem others will want to help you because they see that you care about yourself. When you seek help be clear about what you need and how someone can help.

Your Response:

When you have problems do the following:

1. *Look for the root cause.*
2. *List several solutions.*
3. *Choose the best one given the circumstances and available resources.*

Proverb: Tek time mash ants yu fine im belly

English: If you smash an ant cautiously you will find its
belly

*Interpretation: When you provoke a person you will discover their
anger threshold*

What can you learn?

Try to keep the peace by not doing things to
provoke others to anger or into doing things that
will disturb the harmony already established.

Your Response:

*Write a peace plan of no more than five points to show how to
get along with that person who irritates the clothes off your
back. Implement the plan.*

Proverb: Tek weh yu cyaa get till yu get wat yu want

English: Take what you can get until you get what you want

Interpretation: Make use of every opportunity you get until you achieve your goal

What can you learn?

> Do not refuse anything or opportunity that will take you towards your goal. It matters not if it is small or large.

Your Response:

> *Grab the small opportunities that come your way.*

Proverb: Tideh fi yu, tomarrow fi mi

English: Today for me, tomorrow for you

Interpretation: You may be on top today but I will be on top in the future

What can you learn?

> You will not be on top every day. Life goes in cycles and so you may be better in one area but someone else is better than you in another area. Likewise you may be better off than one person today but that person is better off than you tomorrow. Be prepared to be better than others and for others to be better than you.

Your Response:

> *Be humble in your strengths and weaknesses.*

Proverb: Tief noh lub si tief carry lang bag

English: A. thief does not like to see another thief carrying a long bag

Interpretation: Bad minded people hate to see others flourishing

What can you learn?

Bad minded people will always be envious of others, especially if they think you are doing better than them. Regardless of what they say or do continue to work towards success. Be proud of your accomplishments.

Your Response:

Count your blessings and use them to help others.

Proverb: Tiga ole im drink a rock hole

English: An old tiger will drink at a hole in the rock

Interpretation: The old person cannot do the things he used to do when he was younger

What can you learn?

Maintain a healthy lifestyle regardless of your age, so that you can remain strong and energetic. Eat right, get enough sleep, exercise daily, rest, worship God, read, do puzzles and play with friends and family.

Your Response:

Make a pledge with yourself to maintain a healthy lifestyle from this moment onwards. Research and put a plan in place to do so.

Proverb: Time langa dan rope

English: Time longer than rope

Interpretation: No matter what you do to me time will heal the scars

What can you learn?

> Regardless of what you are going through, it will end in the future. There are lessons to be learnt in the situation, so focus on the lessons you can learn instead of focusing on the painful side of the situation.

Your Response:

> *When you find yourself in a difficult position, focus on the lessons to be learnt.*

Proverb: Wa gaan bad a mawning cyaa come good a evenin

English: What went bad in the morning cannot come good in the evening

Interpretation: We should not worry about a situation that we allowed to deteriorate

What can you learn?

> Be cautious in what you do, if precautions are not taken in the early stages of a project, it will be harder to fix in the later stages; e.g. if the foundations of a house are not laid properly the building will not be safe when it is built and the foundations will be harder to fix later.

Your Response:

> *Lay safe foundations in all your undertakings so that your affairs will be secure.*

Proverb: Want awl, lose awl

English: Want all, lose all

Interpretation: When you try to keep it all to yourself you will lose everything

What can you learn?

When you hoard everything for yourself you will make enemies and will eventually lose it all. Share and use your good fortune to help others.

Your Response:

Identify someone you can lend a helping hand through service. Help that person.

Proverb: Wanti wanti cyan get ih an getti getti noh want ih

English: Want it want it cannot get it and get it get it does not want it

Interpretation: The person who is in need of something cannot get it yet the person who has it has no need of it

What can you learn?

> We do not always get what we want and what we get is not always what we want. We should however learn to be grateful and share what we are able to acquire.

Your Response:

> *At the end of each day find five things for which to be grateful. Your attitude to life will change for the better.*

Proverb: Wa sweet mout hat belly

English: What is sweet in the mouth hurts the belly

Interpretation: Some things that are delightful to us will cause us pain or shame

What can you learn?

Not everything that seems good and appealing is for our good. We must practice to discern those things which only appear to be in our best interest but often cause more harm than good.

Don't envy others for what they have.

Your Response:

Be wise in your decision making. Weigh the pros and con before coming to a conclusion.

Proverb: When man belly full im bruk pat

English: When the man's belly is full he will break the pot

Interpretation: A contented man soon forgets where he is coming from or discomforts he suffered in the past

What can you learn?

Always remember your past. Remember the persons who helped to clear the path for you, those who helped you along the path and those who provided the things you needed to access the path.

Your Response:

Send a personal thank you note to at least one of those persons who helped you along your pathway.

Proverb: When mawga plantin waan dead im shoot

English: When a meagre plantain wants to die it sends out a shoot

Interpretation: When we do not care about our character or safety we do stupid things that could cause us harm

What can you learn?

> Be always aware of the consequences of your action and do only those things that will not bring you into disrepute.

Your Response:

> *Write five reasons why you should be careful of the activities in which you participate.*

Proverb: When rat lub romp roun puss jaw, one day im a goh en up inna puss craw

English: When puss loves to romp around the puss' jaw, one day he will end up in the puss' craw

Interpretation: When you play with danger you will eventually be hurt

What can you learn?

> Being careless in our actions will not help us to succeed and will lead to hurt for ourselves and or our loved ones. Be cautious in your actions.

Your Response:

> *Explain to a younger person why they should not be careless in their actions.*

Proverb: When trouble tek yu pickney shut fit yu

English: When you are in trouble a child's shirt will fit you

Interpretation: When one is in trouble any help offered is appreciated regardless of how small or embarrassing it may be

What can you learn?

All help offered when we are in trouble should be appreciated. We need other people to help us and should therefore treat all persons we interact with, with dignity.

Your Response:

Graciously accept help offered to you.

Proverb: Wilful wase bring woeful want

English: Wilful waste brings woeful wants

Interpretation : Knowingly wasting resources will bring us to painful ends/ needs in the future

What can you learn?

Always be careful in the use of your resources.

Your Response:

Plan carefully how you make use of your resources. Give to others who are in need instead of wasting it.

Proverb: Yiye noh si, heart noh lep

English: Eye do not see, heart will not leap

Interpretation: What you do not know will not hurt you

What can you learn?

There are times when the less you know about a situation the better it will be for your peace of mind. When a situation does not concern you ignore it; unless it will result in harm to you.

Your Response:

Vow not to meddle into affairs that you have not experienced for yourself, especially rumours.

Proverb: Yu cyan siddung pan cow back cuss cow kin

English: You cannot sit on the cow's back and curse cow skin

Interpretation: We shouldn't curse someone on whom we depend

What can you learn?

> Be grateful to those persons who are willing to lend you a hand when you are in trouble or who will help in your development.

Your Response:

> *Always remember to pray for and to say thanks to those persons who offer you a helping hand on life's journey.*

Proverb: Yu cyan ketch Quaku yu ketch im shut

English: You cannot catch Quaku, catch his shirt

Interpretation: If you cannot get to the person who has wronged you, get to someone close to him

What can you learn?

Be careful what you do in life as an innocent person can be hurt because of your wrongdoing.

Your Response:

Do something nice for someone related to a person who has been less than good to you.

Proverb: Yu fraid fi yiye, yu neba nyam head

English: If you are afraid of eyes you will never eat the
head (of edible animals)

*Interpretation: If you place too much value on what others think you
will never be successful*

What can you learn?

Hold your head up high and do what is necessary for
your success. Ignore the doubts that will surface in
your mind about what others will say. Do not listen
to the naysayers, take advice only from persons you
trust to guide you on the path to success.

Your Response:

*Step out of your shell and do that one thing you have been
telling yourself or others have been telling you, that you cannot
do. Just do it.*

Proverb: Yu pred yu bed haad, yu ha fi lidung pan ih haad

English: If you spread your bed hard, you must lie on a hard bed

Interpretation: You must accept the consequences of your actions

What can you learn?

> Whatever you sow you will reap. Sow deeds of kindness, joy, peace, love and goodness so you may reap a life of contentment.

Your Response:

> *Say a kind word to each person you meet today.*

Proverb: Yu shake man han yu noh shake im haat

English: You shake a man's hand but you do not shake his heart

Interpretation: You can see a person's appearance but you cannot tell what is inside the person.

What can you learn?

> Do not judge people by their appearance. Get to know them and discover their true character, by their words and actions.

Your Response:

> *When you meet someone for the first time look beyond the way the person is dressed or groomed. Get to know them before forming an opinion of their worth.*

ABOUT THE AUTHOR

Veronica Sutherland is a Jamaican, who has lived in Jamaica all her life except for a brief stint studying in the United States of America. Veronica has lived in several areas of Jamaica and of such has been exposed to the varied aspects of Jamaican culture.

Her early years were spent at the feet of her maternal grandparents from whom she learnt many things about Jamaican life, including Jamaican proverbs.

This book of Jamaican proverbs is a natural outflow of Veronica's knowledge of and fascination with her beloved homeland.

You may visit her website at:
Healthfulfamilyconversations.weebly.com

PLEASE POST A REVIEW

Now that you have read **'Wisdom From Ole Time Jamaican People'** if you feel others will enjoy reading it or will learn something from it; please return to where you purchased it and leave a review.

Printed in Dunstable, United Kingdom